st. mary at main

st. mary
at main

patrick friesen

For Duncan.
Thanks for the wonderful
poems — they're excellent —
Bére.

Patrick Friesen
april 27/98

The Muses' Company Series Editor: Catherine Hunter
Cover design by Pedro Mendes
Cover and author photograph by Marijke Friesen
Printed and bound in Canada

Published with the assistance of the Manitoba Arts Council and
The Canada Council for the Arts.

The author wishes to thank The Canada Council for the Arts for its support.

The italicized lines in "nomads" are from the introduction to *Aloud: Voices from the Nuyorican Poets Café*. Ed. Miguel Algarin and Bob Holman (Henry Holt, 1994).

Some of these poems were previously published in *Prairie Fire* and *Grain*;
"flood" was commissioned by CBC Radio Manitoba. This piece has also been produced as a commemorative limited edition letterpress poster by award-winning artist Marion Llewellyn of Dream Dead Press.

Canadian Cataloguing in Publication Data

Friesen, Patrick, 1946–
    st. mary at main

Poems
ISBN 1-896239-32-3
    I. Title.
PS8561.R496S35 1998   C811'.54   C98-900113-X
PR9199.3.F77S35 1998

For all the artists of Winnipeg

Contents

A train slips through the city shrouded in a midnight drizzle.

Across the street, inside the Times Change Blues Bar, Big Dave McLean growls through Barbecue Bob, Slim Harpo, and Elmore James.

Bending the strings of his 1932 National. *Atlanta Moan*. Raw. *Raining In My Heart* with a ragged cry. Singing through, singing through. For all of us, on a rainy night.

Traffic sliding by silently. St. Mary at Main.

The harp blowing

the angel wakes

I know the light's on
all night at esther's
and lerner and fournier
are playing at sunstone
I know dave's bending
notes at times change

and the city lives
catching its breath
as towers fall away
and false Gods
shut their gobs

donahue's on corydon
talking with tim
outside heaven
don and carol
on their evening walk
stop at nucci's
who knows what characters
carol's harboring
mcmanus in the west end
shaping a few of his own

the angel wakes
from a troubled sleep
stirring the city alive
into a night of prayer
and dance

I know the light's on
all night in the north end
that music leaks
through two or three doors
where they're gathered
and the wind blows long
down the avenue

raw as light

a city raw as light
like the brutality of birth
a child slipping
into the world
born and stunned

a city on the edge
of the shield
where stone slopes
into the ancient bed
of a long gone lake

a place of imagination
a chimera
or what's left at dawn
of dreams
and memories

holland and treherne

heading in from the southwest
somewhere between holland and treherne
with moments of silent sheet lightning
flaring on the road a thousand miles ahead
and the wind flooding through my car
with the smell of the prairie
I'm singing lit up
you know how it is
earth humming like a machine
and all the answers blown out the windows
nothing left to do
just steering the car like god
straight at winnipeg rising suddenly in the dark
a red neon dome inferno
all the forests of earth aflame
all the hosts of heaven bending to the conflagration
ah there's no way of saying this
any better than it's been said
the song its blood and wind
the human cry of joy and terror
it's been said
it's all been said
how strange strange strange
and swallowed in space

midtown bridge

I don't know why this comes back to me
it was midnight in may 1967
and I was standing on the midtown bridge
throwing money into the assiniboine
$200 it was a test a question of discipline
what comes back is the soft air that night
the liquid ripple of water I could hardly see
dark and silver and beckoning
I think I threw the money in lieu of myself
that was a necessary consideration those days
and across two rivers the beacon of the neon cross
what comes back is the loosening of my shoulders
my body relaxing into an illusion of freedom
thinking for the moment an illusion is as good as the real thing
and walking home with a light step and an empty pocket
not sure now any of this happened
the bridge the river I remember
the rest money and life all a story
long gone fluttering through air

all-night dive

and I say *welcome to winnipeg*
to a gathering of poets
the words suddenly slick and sick
and rotten on my tongue
as if I can welcome anyone
as if this is my city
or I know it
or care for it more than
that

the fraud
of this instrument
the poet
going down in love
playing playing
with every last breath
the city won't be saved
but it'll sound good
and titanic
nearer and nearer
my god

the poem burns
like rust
corrosive and lovely
in the city
a spell to keep us going
those are pearls he says
diving
and he's diving
his flesh
around a breath

and so welcome
to the all-night joint
memory's kind of scarce
these days
you can't buy a dream
welcome
to the all-night
dive

the drummer disappears

hanging out at perkins
endless cups of coffee
or georgie's down the street
with its chainsaw music and beer

waiting for the rock 'n' roll dream
to break out of the factory
out of the suburbs
into the heart of things

drunk on minimum wage
from the fast food joints
trying to get a hook
on the music's volume

this is where music
listens to itself
where everything's raw
and bleeding

this is where cars
jack-rabbit start at the lights
power surging
between brain and foot

a dog on its leash
the city trembles
its pure energy always
about to explode

the music churning
in the jumpy bar
the drummer disappears
inside his time

beneath the streetlamp

my instincts are anarchic
tear down this house
not to begin again
but to be always building
always disappearing

bakunin boulevard
and stirner strasse
becoming becoming
the selves reaching out
like a road

this city collapsing
in its slow ruin
of sewers and electricity
the city grinding
into its own desert

an ambulance
on blocks
hung children
turning beneath
the streetlamp

through the windshield

driving down portage avenue
I'm not sure if it's the hour
7 pm or that it's august
but the street is spread open
and through the windshield
all I see is sky
buildings dwarfed
small dark fronts against the blue
half-erased smudges like low clouds
'the city is low
like it's just broken from the ground
or maybe it's suspended there
by invisible wires
flat as an aircraft carrier or a raft
the city floats here
caught in a magnetic field

and the light streams by the sony billboard
pouring through car windows into my eyes
and there's too much light
with elms lit and shimmering
unbearably into my dilated pupils
and everything begins to look the same
all shadow and light
and I hear the trees like birds singing
buildings rumbling with talk
a soundtrack of auras
but no angels no beating wings
only things fading away
earth's matter seared to light
on portage avenue heading downtown

we don't remember like armenians

we don't remember like armenians
we don't keep the deeper history
no alphabet to save no icons
there are no words that matter

we are only the latest bones
not yet buried or forgotten
our memories are personal
and we are here to make money

our cultures are broken and new
something that didn't work
and no bulwark against nature
its sands drifting through

faint drums are the only music
all the rest passes on
strong steel rails bend easily
beneath the seething sun

corydon avenue coffee

corydon avenue coffee smells italian a hint of old world without
    effort
I wonder how you are my love across the river you always have
    words for me
I'm balanced here for a moment mid-continent winnipeg where
    chaplin played and groucho and king george vi
living in prairie light like pale blue fire living sleeplessly with the
    clarity of a slow dream

at home in bed listening to the rustle of rain outside the slats of my
    venetian blinds
listening to the 2 a.m. train across the assiniboine its low horn and
    its heavy wheels
there'll be another soon and then the robins will be awake singing
    in the backyard
and it's a moment that pretty well holds everything I want to say
    about what's lost and not
holds everything just long enough for me to want to say it then
    scatters out of the emptiness it's been

living this heart attack on dead-end road looking through the city
    for the one who names the streets
listening for the note that rises between nostalgia and the hard facts
    of time
passing through endless intersections the night lit with traffic

doors

the doors here
where do they lead?
a door into the land
into the idea of a city

the borders here
each street a frontier
around the block
around the world

histories piled
on top of each other
mingled stories
air and air

the january taste
of a black beechnut cough drop
fowler's falafel
at the *pure lard cafe*

cowie's fine lectures
in the tier building
gathering chalkdust
all over himself

brask reading
the new bio on brecht
a navajo ring
on his heart finger

eating humous at *winona's*
wanting to rub a circle
on the steamed windows
or write my name

umbilical city

this is a city of muscle
the nation's heart
a city that sends its blood
pumping toward both coasts
this is a city of origins
nestled in granite
omphalos lenny named it

a city that births you
a city you have to leave
to survive
and arrive at
to die
alone

this is not a city that mourns
it is too busy being born

this is a city of visions
you don't pass through lightly
the city of wiseman and proch
livesay and breau
their echo on the famished streets

an umbilical city
that draws its offspring back

where lenny anderson
leapt from his tower
to the street

o'connell with rumi on his mind
picking *amazing grace*
on his cheap stella guitar

hart pivoting in the stillness
winnipeg shuffling its feet outside

on the corner of dominion and westminster
staring at her old home
gwendolyn looking for her dog
or waiting for a letter
gwendolyn who never left
though she moved away
toward her desert dreams
of water

this is a city that doesn't mourn
a crux of energy
and time held still
the wheel spinning in clay
and ghosts rising from the marsh
a good place
for a poet
to remember the dead

the eye

here in this city
with its water and wide sky
you look through the clear eye
of the continent

there is no mystery here
eagle is called
and materializes from air
no angels doctor but in things

you stand there human
against the horizontal light
sky fills the streets
and you drift away

this city is hardly here
only a tough mirage
an oasis for nomads
drawn to its radiant core

light dances like rain
on a cloudless day
feels like speed and wired
all morning long

then it's twilight
the sun flaring rose
and brilliant as hallucinations
over st. james

the eye a warm eye
and the pulsing heart
of a tender city
dressed for work

this is how the streets are wired

donahue on corydon
dressed with elegance
his hair grey past his gifts
eyes round like a spooked horse
he's got rent to raise
and living on cucumbers and water
I'm wishing he could tune up
right there on the sidewalk
but he's pawned his guitar
and I miss his irish tenor

what is it some spirits do with their grace?
resisting the full circle
like they can't handle too much
the wiring's all wrong
and they've electricity sparking off their hands
their hair on fire their eyes borrowed from a crazy dream

and others drink their way out of bodies
burning through to the smoke of soul
and always in the morning
crumpled once more in their charred flesh
the romance long gone
some find words in talk or the keyboard
slithering out of their skins and hunger
into the night's beauty
golden bodies adrift until morning
with the scrawl to answer for
the utter risk the scratchings in the light of day

and donahue is at the heart of this city
even without his guitar
and his voice vanishing
he's come through
to name the streets he walks
his conversations at intersections
touching the city like a current
this is how the streets are wired

and we could all be heading for the riverbank
newspaper mattress waiting for us
and thinking it's christmas morning with blue snow
and bells and no traffic on osborne bridge
and it's anyone's place on the assiniboine
lost and sentenced to this
an old coat falling from my shoulders
and saying so long like a tin whistle
down the road

forgetting into the city

a midden
the scraps of a refugee camp
these fish bones
these streets
this double city
of ghost and muscle

down water avenue
across the provencher bridge
to gabrielle roy's lost street

safarik at riel's grave
staring at the stars
above the stone ruin of the cathedral
he raises a bottle
to the glassy trees
while the cemetery howls

nuns like dark ships
drifting down taché
smiling left and right
their hands working beads
carpenters straddling a roof beam
and spitting nails
shingles flying through the air
someone at a piano
inside an open window

all bunched muscle and nerve
this city is tough and ecstatic
bachman's guitar skittering
like a spider on water
into *shakin' all over*
lenny breau strumming his guitar
in some club on carleton
lerner playing *news travels fast in the desert*
how we find our way here for a while
among the elm and the oak
wandering through our lives
trying to leave something behind
evidence a voice a breath

and I'm back with the scraps
looking for the words of this city
I'm back with safarik's bottle
and the lovely one
with silver at her wrists
opening the word
inside my heart

orange moon

an orange moon hanging
like a swollen womb over notre dame
I'm waiting for it to groan
the silent city sleeping in december

the weight of this night
a quilt a long long sleep
wherever takes you in
when you disappear

what do you want?

a telephone ringing all night
behind the walker theatre
a rolled-up sock on the curb
light falling from a donut shop

an old woman on her knees
looking for something at the intersection
or praying crazy
her arms opening to the street

what does she want?

who knows where souls hide
beneath frayed winter coats
the city struggling
to breathe through the night

you can hear its emphysema
in that rasping sleep
you can hear the distant thud of trains
shunting in winter yards

what do they want?

I wonder if they'll find us
frozen beneath the ice
digging out this lonely city
from its long sleep

the swollen moon dreams
of ancient travails
births and cries
where the wind still blows

what does it want?

marlene dietrich didn't live here

marlene dietrich didn't live here
edith piaf or lotte lenya
nothing that well-dressed and world weary
I never saw modigliani asleep on the boulevard
an empty bottle and a shabby suit
the man could charm a pigeon
didn't see him the night he walked all night
down parisian streets with akhmatova
just saw photographs of her various rooms
and his drawing in the background
an elegance on bare soviet walls
he didn't make love in this city
no shows at the plug in gallery

no ottoline morrell no garsington
and no jacques brel what a shame
no giacometti no camus or cocteau
the endlessness of european names
smothering their cities and cafes
with delicacies pomposity and delights
loaves of french bread and airie confections
play and more play so many years of pretending
and we're just beginning

this ain't chicago

this ain't chicago with its tracks and brawn with its sandburg muscle
and rhythm this is two rivers passing through the resurrection

this ain't the mississippi delta with its dark despair giving voice with
its robert johnson betrayal this is a bled city shifting over a graveyard

this ain't vienna with lotte lenya in the alley with cabaret in its blood
this is where the ghosts are waiting as the rain dance dies

this ain't the city of classics with its tophats and sonatas with its
measured step this is the desolation of bingo halls and socials

this ain't cairo with its minarets and nile with disaster on its calendar
this is the stardust motel filled with tourists

this ain't the desert with its absence and miracles with its bedouin wind
this is a postcard without a name

homeless

we are ophelias and lears
we are starlings and purple strife
beautiful in our homelessness
a white wind from another land
the falling seeds of manna
we are the heroes of our imagination
dreaming winnipeg where the rivers meet
and building our stage there

come now that we live here
it is long time we turn
and work our way into other imaginations
heroes become brutal
grimacing in their awful masks
heroes are blind missionaries
martyrs to what they no longer see
and executioners of what they never saw

we are lears on the plains
storms around our mad decisions
we are orphans
wandering ever farther from home
a trail of shoes behind us
old clothes and masks
barefoot finally on the stage
with nothing to say

the forks

walking through the forks
I don't see anyone that belongs
a traveller in my own town
but then I always was

I don't know the red river
a muddy strand
running along the spine
of america
I don't know its cowboys and indians
or its pioneers
I'm watching the geese fly
I'm listening to the blues

this isn't home
it's a city I've come to
without expectations
on my way home
pausing here for children
the assiniboine at the end of the street
stopping for lilacs in june

provencher bridge

from the bridge
you can see the cross
looming through the night
basilica's starry wheel
turning in the sky
from the bridge
you can remember
the prairie
at the end of provencher

suzanne lives there
she's peeling an orange
suzanne from le havre
montreal or brest
suzanne with her dark braid
and blue eyes

she's the stranger
across the river
the other one
there's so much between us
words and icons
all the gold and rubble
of nations

we live like that
with our different ways
how we genuflect or not
how we speak or dance
where our ships came from
we live like that
meeting on the bridge
some moonlit nights
the river glittering
beneath us

blood is so thick
the dream of home so deep
and here we live
never quite home
feeling betrayed
and abandoned
on both sides of the river
a mirage of canoes
slipping through the water
and the distant shouts
of barter

backbone beat

thinking of other places
other streets and names
remembering what I don't know
other songs other ways

it's how I know this place
looking at it from away
new york copenhagen
it's how I place this place
its workmen and keepers of time
young women who pass for a moment
at portage and main
and descend underground
this is the city that should have given its keys
to charlie watts
that backbone beat
upon which anything can happen

the edge of things here
the shield butting at our shoulder
the lake we live in
this is all risk and sudden death
we keep drumming
so we won't perish on the edge of the prairie
our trains rumbling through the nights
we keep drumming
so the northern lights won't overwhelm us
we build our music against the sky
that drumbeat
and our improvisation at the edge

march 4/66

snow to the eaves
and a vanished city
white and clean as paper
before the story is written

a torn paperback
fallen from a rider's pocket
its leaves fanning in the wind
page by page drifting into the city

a familiar story of greed
the legends of heroism
an ancient plot coming down
on a simple family

it's always stormed like this
the blindness of blowing snow
the rider gone mad
and the horse frozen in its harness

we've always known this futility
our eyes hardened by hope
everything vanishes
and we never find our way home

january

wind funnels down sturgeon creek
across portage avenue
like a northern blade
some mongolian scythe
sweeping across the world
and you're knee-deep
and plunging ahead
for the impossible bus shelter
caught to the bone

you're ancient
a walker and crawler of snow
an old one alone
and adrift
mazed in the perfect infinity
of a wednesday morning
in january
frantic to belong
to someone or something
anything
to light the candle of your heart

this is a month of despair
nothing behind you
and nothing ahead
just a brain-damaging wind
and this amnesia of cold cold cold

and yet
it's too easy
this saying of something true
the unbearable cold is a fire
that sears skin
enfolds the drunk
behind the hotel
it is too easy
to remember hooves and sleds
too easy to remember
tongues frozen to door knobs

you're tempered
in the frost and fire
of this city
tempered and hard
as the shield
at your right hand
the shoulder of stone
where hawks pillage
small life

you're tempered here
pale as snow
caught in europe's story
lurching above
buried tools and bones
tempered
among the towers
and broken streets
of this house

april

you think this is it
the sun in your hair
your jacket flung open?
you think it's done
the flooding river
diminishing
within its banks?

march has gone
with its pale wind
and ice floes
your lawn's
revealed its dogshit
its dead sparrows
and letters

you think april
is always the month
of resurrections?
come
I'll light a fire
and tell you tales
of betrayal

between the window and the sky

muscle the long line won't say it
rhythm running out to the horizon
the vanishing point of story
everything shaking down

haiku
gesundheit

and nothing more to say

a spoon on the sill glinting for a second
television murmuring down the hall
no one lives here
chet baker singing *imagination* on someone's radio

kerouac said it for a while
tried to say it like a long breath
straddling the wheel
and breaking broncos

lenny anderson had the rap
and the sunken eyes
he walked the talk
whistling up the stairs
and diving off the roof

nothing happened
between roof and alley
a moment of thought
an image that might have surprised him
who knows?

nothing happens
between arthur and albert
a few hookers on long legs
leaning into red camaros
and pickup trucks
driving round and round
nothing happens

lenny talked like gold
glittering on the walls of a mind
his mind a cage of pain
and not many jailbreaks
his eyes on death

a spoon on the sill
in a late jazz afternoon
kelly hears him heading up the stairs
singing to himself
the creak of a step
a voice disappearing at the top
nothing happens
not in the roaring black holes of heaven
not beneath the archway on arthur
where the graffiti says *set me free*

nothing happens
between the window and the sky
no long steel rails no muscle
the mapmakers have only charted
the territories of their own minds

lenny flat-out
in an alley off princess street
last breath the stars he breathed
slipping silently from his mouth
returning somewhere
he never reached
and nothing happens
the necessary vanity
of the mind
shaping despair
the radio and the stairs
into something
that broke with him

no kerouac jazz

tonight doesn't feel like anything
holding the city together
no kerouac jazz
nothing tearing through the heart
running all the way through
the city impaled on a note
nothing's working tonight
the city festering like a bomb
a refugee camp
a raft going down
looking for some noise
a sound to call god out

big dave cuts through the fog
on a good night
with greenwood mississippi in his heart
playing for a moment
that this is the crossroads
this city this valley
that something happens here
trains and malone beside the tracks
and janet and esther and per
and my love with silver
at her wrists
but it isn't mississippi
not tonight
no way of saying us
for long
this city's story
a held breath on the prairie

an old scratchy 78 audiodisc
with ma singing *holy city* in 1949
that's a route somewhere
not the song nor the faith
but the young voice
yearning into a dream of jerusalem
a sister ghost
yearning into the fervent story
toward streets of gold

holy city
of one-eyed visions
sword gallows and olives
the word at large
world spinning
into this city
boxcars rusting along the red
broken ploughs and corrals
this windy city
with its lost human song
muttering downtown
among thistles and bricks

a sacred midden
beneath the streets
says who?
archaeologist
with the memory of a sieve
singer
without a style
words come easy
easy go
memory
between the lines
the furrows and curbs
says who?
the dead
with their truthful tongues
and nothing but style

seems so silent down there
when you don't have the ears
and me gesturing
with my european hand
looking for some broken notes
something to find my heart
that restless immigrant
without a passport

and there's the lovely one
walking along the bay

nomads

the hard humour
and relentless easy obscenities
the mad admiration for crackheads
and the everlasting wars of whitey and nigger
man and woman
rage and obscenity as terror
no open hearts
because there are knives and greed
and fear and snow everywhere
because somewhere
hidden away is the last shock
tenderness

making sacred
junkies and killers
so much callous and brutal
a cool way
out of pain

the centre is here
in winnipeg with its heat
and skies a clarity
the centre is not new york city
turning on itself
on its innocence
in its exhaustion
thin-skinned faces
always ready to tear through
shaping the face volcanic

the soul
sunken
into the dig
the soul
gone archaeological
a butterfly pinning itself
into the collection

I am a barbarian here on the lower east side
a barbarian of some middle way
of balance and love
going nowhere
a brute without ideology
winnipeg man
with memory on the brain
and old ways

the long stride
hands
the path

always I am the way
that's still running in my veins
the coming and the going
and the ceremony of each

the nomad gone to ground in winnipeg
via ukraine poland and the lowlands
the nomad without fields
without mountains to cross
the nomad without a way
gone to poetry
here
this city
poet with 600,000 words
a language he wasn't born into
poet with his senses about him
an empty mirror
and the desire to love

and yes
another
on the lower east side
with the streets
beneath his feet
a poet
whose ashes
they spread
from houston to 14th street
from second avenue to the mighty D

calling out
it's miky piñero
and it was
his ashes
claiming the path
a nomad
always going home

st. michael & all angels

living this heart attack of a life on these streets tonight passing st.
   michael and all angels church
stone and low beneath dark trees almost an outpost a barracks a
   corner of england famous and mildewed
high anglican dust and elegance and thomas hardy in the shade
   with angel clare and eustachia vye

a ghost on the street corner and the beautiful voices of traherne and
   vaughan and herbert
wandering through heaths kings and daughters and barefoot
   tinkers buried in barrows
webster's genius the howl of a heavy note his unlidded eyes looking
   to the darkness within

all the words and rhythms are rain or wind a common book of
   prayer or john donne from the pulpit
it's what we speak here on most of these streets at least a bastard
   child with too many words
and the ghost stands there with his tuxedo wilting at the sleeves
   with the smell of rose water and daffodils

god's stench

god's stench on balmoral
an old man snoring on a bench
gulls gliding across the gallery's prow
gasoline hazing off asphalt

my son's shopping for fashion
in the army surplus store
I'm watching for suicides
to dive splashing off the bay

sometimes there's too much light
or maybe that's not it
sometimes the eyes are too wide open
and all earth's light flares in

sometimes the world is unbearable
the city lit like an explosion
the steel and glass and trees
blurred in blazing auras

even the traffic is silent
and there is no necessity for memory
light pouring through
like the first day

brain is sucked out
through my eyes
and imagination vanishes
like sweat

it's god's stench everywhere
and I can't see a thing
I've never been this awake
I watch myself sleep

the gulls swoop in from yesterday
the streets are filled with nostalgia
a mother calls her children
but her children never come

waiting for the flood

dark tracks trestle
where the rivers meet
stone pillars rooted in ice

and a northern wind
driving thin skeins of snow
swirling across the walk

all around cheap towers and glass
and the city crumbling
to grey rubble and broken pavement

the banks give way slowly
at the junction
collapsing into the rivers

we're dragging our bones
into the new century
where no one dies and no one's born

everyone waiting for another chance
for another coming
everyone waiting for the flood

the wheels

tonight I cannot bear the sound of trains
they are not approaching
nor are they passing by
their hard wheels roll away

I can't bear the stairs
walking up and down all night
to say a few words
and leave them behind

leaving and returning and leaving

I don't know where I am tonight
I have lost west from east left from right

snorri brings my shoe in his jaw
I know what he wants
but I can't break from the mirror

nothing moves inside my head

I have loved
I remember that
I have been loved

my heart hurts
like a human stone
and I can't bear the trains

the wheels
grinding
down the line

inner city

listening for the deep song
with its yearning
rooted in its pain
listening for something
like the blues
the jazz of this city
and there's nothing to hear
during the day
nothing to hear
something almost not there
at night in the inner city
something beyond pain and anguish
that cannot be heard
nothing is possible with anguish
nothing but more anguish

the young hang themselves from trees
you can't hear their voices
and the drums are still

listening for the human voice
listening for its range
its wickedness and beauty
letting it go letting it go

what's the story natalya

it's dark downtown natalya everyone standing around waiting for
    something
blades and naked children fixed on sugar cardboard windowpanes
    and a door on one hinge
there's nothing but cutlery on the table and television's blue light
    on the wall
someone on the corner playing with a bullet in his pocket and a
    mirror in his hand

it's raw in this city hunger and angry jazz in the veins streetlamps
    without light
walking on reeboks and glass a 24 in a baby carriage evening matins
    about to begin
there's nothing to do no one's working for the body no one's working
    for the soul
it's all broken down there's no tenderness in the alley no tenderness
    on broadway

how to say this it's all crooked it's all turned around how to tell you
    the phone is bugged
people waiting for someone to say *come along with me* people
    waiting for some christ
the street cleaner's caught in the crossfire on main street stocks are
    shooting through the roof
even god's tired and looking for the messiah anything to get him out
    of here

and baby it's so wonderful your natural tan the lord and the beast
    in the street
how do we make it through the day when there's no heart for it no
    longing?
not waiting for anything though something's got to happen or
    something's going to give
someone's on the corner playing with a bullet and the mirror's
    flashing in the sun

so what's the story natalya how do we get out of here where do we
    find our shoes?
looks like no one knows where they're standing anymore looks like
    no one cares
let's go for a walk the two of us I think I love you but I'm not sure
    in the rain
I want to ask the man for his bullet but I know what's in the mirror

still life

from the air
the city is a diamond
of cold blue lights
the molten copper and heaviness
of a three-quarter moon
hanging from heaven

november snow
drifts hard as confetti
against the curb
but there's no wedding
no celebration
no birthday anywhere

and there's no music
the window's dark
someone's covered
a doorknob
with a found glove
reaching out

looking for forgiveness
isn't that the way?
the city in its sins
smoke sagging
like a still life
above the frozen red

looking for tamerlane

looking for the village idiot to raise this city to the clouds
looking for the old woman who sings hymns on the corner
looking for the one who walks by the river

I'm looking for tamerlane
with his red red sword

looking for the dishevelled woman with her black hair and bracelets
looking for the drunk who knows his drunkeness with a shrug
looking for anna with a shawl of roses on her shoulders

I'm looking for tamerlane
with his red red sword

looking for the city beneath this city
looking for the river of god
looking for the fire

I'm looking for tamerlane
with his red red sword

looking for the grace of light and life and death
looking for the red heart and the blue wind
looking for the angel to carry me away

I'm looking for tamerlane
with his red red sword

looking for the dawn
looking for the city becoming light
looking for an end to the dreams

along the rails

walking along the rails
always from a vanishing point
a farmhouse a tilting barn
the cairns and cemeteries
where we've been

walking along the rails
always on the horizon
the spine of some sardonic beast
laurier's whistle stops
and european immigrants

walking along the rails
always toward a vanishing point
wishing for colville's horse
a pushcart a comet anything
something out of eternity

eternities

the rebbes and children
the stalking stag
of warkov's territory
the fetus-faced dolls
just fallen from heaven
her perfect birds and fish
caught out of their elements
baba's on burroughs or machrae
her familiar old old world

we sit here at kelekis
exchanging the cliches
of our separate eternities
and the hotdogs are good
the fries not as good as the myth
all those north end heroes
staring at us from the walls
and esther in her tenderness
could lacerate anything in her path
because it's there
a kind of ceaseless mountain climbing
and you've got to laugh
with her quicksilver mind
listening to true anarchy

I've never figured what frightens her
maybe the world at large
or the usual ma and pa disasters
but it doesn't matter
I love her talk and wit
her nighttime forays of work
and there's no doubt she's reached
from her eternity
down into these west kildonan streets
and made something that kisses time
I recognize it but can't say much
only laugh with her
waiting for heaven

lilacs

lilacs
that's what
a brevity
a mauve frost in may
in this city of rivers
in this flood

blow wind

valour road

listen listen
in a quiet july afternoon 1934
boys playing catch on valour road
only it's not called that yet

do they dream at night?
the squalor and pain
their possible heroism
a bomber flailing through a dark sky

listen to the whispering
unimaginable violence
the brawn of nations gathering
listen to the mutter
of machines
revving in the grove

which of them will join
the maggot cities in france or holland?
whole underground cities
unmapped streets and squares
cities without tongue
where you never go lost

listen to the tremor
along the rails
your ear to the steel
what is in those heavy cars?

the boys perfecting spit balls
the evening so long
and the summer an eternity
on valour road

trains

at night
I tell time by trains
a distant diesel
the rumble of its wheels
from a mile away
across the assiniboine
through my window
I tell time
once in a while
the european engine
sixteen coaches
ghosting through the city
in the utter dark
I tell time
in the station
waiting for word
from away

a train is the distance grief travels
singlehearted and relentless
the weight of horizon
on a standing man
it is forgotten terrain
shifting from birth to birth
a train never comes around
it returns the way it went

trains pass
through the city's sleep
being dreamed
like rivers
like memory
with its freight
I tell time by trains
old stories riding the rod
through the night

caught in the city

there's a drummer
at the heart of the house
there's a river
in the basement

tonight what I want
and what I am
are not the same
my feet in the creek
my hands in the air
the red-winged blackbird's song
is my soundtrack
each day airplanes
drone through it
I'm here with a dog
on a leash
and a speeding ticket
on the dash

caught in the city with my words
I'm asking where you are
I hear your bracelets
silver on your slender wrists
you find your way
into everything I say

a watery place

we stand at the intersection
jostled and asleep
staring at the lights

we walk through doorways
looking for things
or vaguely remembering

granite seething beneath the city
loose roots and gumbo
earth's first furnace

the city adrift
like an island
on a fiery lake

this is a watery place
a place of second sight
and the hidden flood

a place of burials
old weapons and paper
long forgotten bones

we climb into soft beds
on our way
to nagging dreams

we walk on water
all day
at night we drown

rabbit

I try to name
the rabbit
that crosses
my backyard
every day

small and brown
beside the tin shed
his long ears
swivelling toward me
I think
he wants
a conversation

and he remains
motionless
as I crouch
slowly
three feet away
his ears alert
his narrow body shivering

just when
I wonder
if something
is passing
between us
and I gently reach
for him
he's gone

in the winter
his tracks
litter the snow
especially
in the hollow
wind has carved
around the berry bush

I see him less
then
as if he's been
drawn
into the landscape
or
down the hole
to hades

I can't name him
or her
this isn't a film
or story
and some things
remain unnamed
even in the culture
of the backyard

and yet
some days
when I step
from the back door
he's there
tremulous
and still
in the open snow

thorkkelson glass

my friend paul says
once you see the light of greece
you understand its philosophers
he's from nafplion
and swears by its sky
our light is clear
thorkkelson glass
with blue clouds shimmering inside
and bare branches scratching the horizon
with their calligraphy
our light is not human
not shaped nor interpreted
this is a cool light
a blue silk umbrella
arching over the city
as light as whispers
in the tent of the world

white dog

tonight I'm walking the dog
along sturgeon creek
and everything's fine
it's one of those moments
the first and the last day
when nothing's named
and nothing's lost
there's nothing like october rain
a drizzle in the night
and a white dog
sifting among the rushes
without a whisper
the water silent

the well

looking for the well
where a willow remembers
its roots

letting go

letting go on sherbrook street
encountering the usual violations
my car window smashed once again
shards all over the front seat
maps and identities sprung from the glove compartment
music wrenched from the dash
well why not?
there's not a thing I own in the world

glass glittering around me
in a mirage of streetlights
night rushing through the window
with the gasoline and lilacs of the suburbs
the soft shrapnel of a thousand lives
I'm dead meat in my car
wondering how many have been knifed
with words or blades
how many thrown down the stairs
how many are in love

losing my name in st. james
as the air slings cool and sharp through the car
ainslie moray and wallasey
there are stars falling all over the place
and streetlights and broken glass
and gangs are afoot
looking for someone to tuck them in
and sirens wail in transcona and charleswood
weaving us together with fear

georgie's

my ears bleeding
from the wall of music
at georgie's
and the rum going down fine
more smoke than air
my life flashing before my eyes
barb the neighbour lady
from across the alley
joins me at my table
she's known things
I may not know
about my life
but too decent to spread it
and we're shouting
into each other's ears
stories about our children
remembering them at five
barebacked in the summer
or skating at the rink
down the street
I tell her michael was always the rebel
in her brood
and she knows it
she laughs
tells me some story
of niko at three feet tall
and I turn from her
to watch him on stage
nailing the music to the floor
shirtless and impeccable
in his timing
all six feet of him
hunched over the snare
both feet pounding the pedals
and his eyes lost somewhere
between everything

until they shift to jamie
some imperceptible signal between them
and they bring it all down
niko shivering the cymbals
and I tell barb something or other
about jimmy her oldest
or remembering marijke
dancing beneath the green apple tree
we order another rum each
she asks if it's okay if she smokes
and I can hardly see her
through the smoke
so it seems okay
I mean it won't really be the last nail
in my coffin
and the boys are rocking up there
it's so tight and loose
how else can I put it
I used to live like that too
still do sometimes but it's different now
it's not that wild joy of eternity
it's sadder a kind of quiet sorrow
unfettered and not wanting to go anywhere
like a tree's freedom to stay rooted
death's right there
feel its breath some nights
my hands at the typer
my eyes inside
a hitch in my breathing
a pause between heartbeats
thinking of everything that's died
all the love and leaves the gone chances
words echoing in my ears
still hearing all those voices
their work and laughter and pain
grandfather father and father
the sorrow that's always there
the abandoned heart
that brief moment a fling really
dancing with arms flying
the smell of lilacs in june

the warm dirt of a country road
a fling a sword dance a shuffle
all of it the whole works
and the music's got me pinned
to the world and heaven on its way
I gotta go barb the band's done
and everyone's grown old

ellice avenue

among the used furniture shops italian clubs laundromats and
    german corner groceries two wandering ghosts
my two-year-old daughter riding high on my shoulders her fists
    clutching my hair my hands loosely circle her ankles
1975's sun slanting into my squinting eyes her bare legs brown and
    round with power
my dear it's twenty years done and you're back in this city and it
    feels like I'm on my way gone

it's easy to let nostalgia seep in a man's life disappearing his daughter
    almost his age now
you know what I mean how time differs for them so much faster for
    him than it was so much brighter
the way a photograph fades to brilliance a woman's dark hair flaring
    to white fire around her face
it's so easy to vanish into memory slipping from body into mind into
    thin air into light

it's a still-life those blocks a frozen blur of motion us walking through
    our lives
the body remembers the heat the summer swish of traffic the sounds
    of portuguese and german
the body is a memory of landscapes europe and asia gutturals and
    sibilant whispers of history
an old man with his medals maria at the window her nose flattened
    to the glass

all is flesh and the shadow I used to be sloughed skin on sticks
    following me around
there's eternity a rotten concept if ever the blackbird in the marsh as
    my soul
feathered and small-boned on a cattail and swaying in a slow
    northern wind
doesn't matter marijke because it's enough to be here in the
    improbability of this world

and we're not long for it no one is maria disappears from her
  window the old man already forgotten
they still sell used furniture they play cards in the clubs but the
  corner store is vietnamese
brides still stand on the top steps of their porches waiting for the
  cameras to flash
my shoulders have rounded since 75 but I still feel your fine ankles
  in my hands

quick and dark as a crow

sturgeon creek's high tonight
and the moon is cold
the rain across the water
wants to be snow

driving into the heart of the city
to the times change blues bar
to find the wildness I've been
another side to the road
going blind with song
son house and muddy waters
coming through like strays
how they let themselves go
and I've been blind before
I know how it goes
feeling my way
quick and dark as a crow

the harmonica wailing
a blowing wind
then sliding low
as a bellering hound
there's thunder in the fields
and crickets beneath the porch
someone's walking out of town
there are mirages on the road

strange this music
that's been travelling so long
it's got feet without a home
feels like sorrow
that hardly remembers
where it came from
and doesn't know where it's going

just moaning and growling
here in this city
unquiet spirits from the delta
shuffling down the street
bleeding dark blood
from their old wound
in the morning they're gone

there's nothing but
a quiet sunday street
and that muffled drumbeat
rising at the forks
talking skin
and slow dragging feet
there's nothing but
a ghost dance
where the rivers meet

heart of the city

they're dancing
in the heart of the city
in the heart of the continent
on qu'appelle or cumberland
among the broken bodies
and hung children
or drunk and reeling
down henry
hookers high and skinny
on martha street
is it the last dance
to the last song?
the street filling
with customers

turn out the lights

it's lonely downtown
shadows in doorwells
holding their breaths

the moon at night
doesn't heal
night drips with poison

buildings die
boarded up and papered over
an echo of voices

eaton's or the gaiety
and the old
shoeshine man

a street of knives
losing all memory
in endless repetition

nothing can be done
it's criminal
no matter where you look

turn out the lights
bury your dead
and dig up the map

flood

we know it will come rolling along like rumours from the south
   word of mouth you stop and hold your breath to listen and think
   you hear it like gossip or stories a distant rumble of water but
   there's only a gentle wind playing with the silence
we know it will come like a forgotten promise we wait stunned in a
   dream looking for signs of miracle looking for something we can
   do we build walls around our houses and we wait and wait and wait
we know it will come blood flowing in our veins like swelling rivers
   the earth our body we melt into it with our anxieties we return to the
   earth and its ways stripped of culture and sophistication standing
   with hands at our sides

what are we? old questions rise with the water our strangeness on
   earth our separation and our dominion waters rise and nudge us
   toward memory we shrug it off but fear seeps through something
   unnamed and concealed
what have we done? the red river is rolling toward us in disorder and
   disease an impending judgement the river spreading across fields a
   distant glitter of light relentlessly surrounding us

and then it arrives cresting against our bulwarks all bloated and bitter
   with its cargo of beasts carrying our filth and the death of factories
   bones rolling in the water our history haunting us the drownings the
   sunken ships
it rolls through towns and cities a violent baptism a punishment of the
   planet houses and sheds tilting downstream trees uprooted
   civilization a thin wall of sandbags and the desperation of the
   human animal with its reason its cunning and prayer
the river rolling through our world of words and architecture bursting
   through laws and assumptions

in the end it's a story told by an old man on a bench remembering and
waiting for his end it's biblical because we name it this story of
dogged restlessness

in the end we are displaced so easily not a judgement not a punishment
but simply the way the earth moves and we scratch at the surface
leaving our marks and our bones

in the end no one walks on water we claim our property and close our
eyes in sleep the river returns to its narrow bed and waits

place louis riel

she is all beautiful naked at the window the gauzy curtains around
    her as she gazes across the city
she watches a slow train slip the snowy banks of the river the basilica
    open to the stars
she has blessed this room with her scent the soul of her trembling
    with fine strength
she is elegance in a tough city the care with which she moves through
    the world

from this window you can see the city open out to the prairie steel
    rails vanishing
the dawson trail with its ghosts and whisky jacks almost lost beneath
    snow
madame gaboury and the grey nuns and hanged louis buried across
    the river
but here this woman in the flesh what has always been with us a lover
    and a ghost

at night when the muscle sleeps when the rough hand lies on white
    cotton sheets
in the dark after the day's deals when love and rage fester behind
    the drapes
she moves through the streets breathing for us and making angels in
    the snow
she calls on what's best in us touching the frost at our windows and
    the shoe at the door

incense for the lord

running late with the blue torpedo in my blood looking for sleep for
   something to recall
that's how it goes here in st. james the sun long down and birds
   asleep in the trees
straying toward the garden the old woman still stooped there
   among the peas her hands adrift
it's an irish temptation this borderland where the flesh goes up in
   smoke an incense for the lord

longing for flight this dead weight unshackled for the night diving
   off a stone wall
it's my house foundering here on woodhaven a husk my bones gone
   to ground skinned and quick
dreaming like the shakes thin walls breached to that terrain I've
   come from and return to when I can
that's how it is with the body I adore it its gates and windows
   sprung open I love to leave

breathing in the serene flame of the body's ardour flesh on fire with
   its hunger and thirst
it's the lord moving in mysterious ways writhing through the throes
   of creation
exhaling like death the breath funnelling out to its end the blue
   torpedo riding home
that's how it goes here in this room the body's smell everywhere its
   words and convulsions

a man taking leave of this city

in the heat of july
clouds drifting past the nassau apartments

a busker at osborne and river
singing *hey mr. tambourine man*

a kid with a nose ring
washing windshields
when the light turns red

a tall daughter
striding along osborne
above the prairie

going dizzy
when he stands up
the city reeling for a moment

driving down river and wellington
heading for the maryland bridge
green elms towering like umbrellas

always the clouds adrift
across the world
deepening the sky

there are no angels but these

and the wind
passing through

at night in his kitchen
a man watching moths crawl
through a hole in the screen

watching night's dark foliage
in the back yard
a breath at the window

a man taking leave

wild geese

all day wild geese gathered and circled
tonight I saw them flying
across the moon

big dave meets stephane grappelli

all that room
where the buffalo roamed
horizon at your feet
the sky billowing
like a parachute overhead
coming down hard
the emptiness of gods
gone to seed

the stubble field is silent
with crickets
the city's horizon piling up
like other cities like babel
breaking the skyline

violin bows sway like grass
in an orchestra on parole
a blue train pulling in
with its southern freight

and who would have thought it
the possibilities of music
big dave smoking up
with stephane grappelli
in the can at the concert hall
a little blues a little jazz
and all that room

st. mary at main

walking through the city's terrain
its grids and maps
its money and electricity
walking toward times change
and bev's smile at the door

I love to sit at the window
watching the trains go by
quarter moon hanging there
like a broken clock
and I've got the time

isaac's rolling a mellow cigarette
blues woven into the tension of his hands
always playing beneath what he feels
batting a slow eye as he reaches back

dave's feeling his way
through the night
his silver guitar
strung with dark strings

the city getting drunk
on saturday night
the city teetering
between savagery and bliss
there's so much
to drink away
so much to drink toward
everyone looking for good news
trying to break through
the blue glass of heaven
there's all that love
on the streets
you can see it brawl
its way into forgetfulness

main street's so thirsty
no one gets enough
dreaming toward sunday morning
the hungry ones
hoping for manna
the power and glory
amen and selah
the loners who have seen god
and gone poor

and there's no way for the nomad
the paths have all been paved
and it's the separation
of heart and brain
and everyone's insane
shadows beneath streetlamps
bodies lurching through doorways
we're all silhouettes in the window
trying to make ends meet
body and soul

as they say
keeping the wolf from the door
the blues at 1 a.m.
dave squinting beneath his cap
watching everything
the shuffle
everyone a step closer
or farther from god
home for a moment
in the song
and the voice's desire
the world here
at st. mary and main
a train ghosting by
and the brakeman looking back

the moon in the streets

tonight the moon's sunk into the city
and all the houses are shadows
I thought I wanted to break down walls
but I just want to turn from the snow

I want no one's death but my own
the clarity of a struck piano key
the fabric of a plucked string
I want no other life than this

everyone's walking in someone else's shoes
the heart disorders the world
love's mayhem and sorrow drifting
with the moon in the streets

music through an open door
the heat of the room billowing out
I see her dancing on the floor
here at the heart of things

it's st. mary at main
where you forget everything
nothing being born
but the light

lovely one

all night
I dreamed her
the lovely one
with a silver
bracelet
on her wrist

she sang
with me
about rivers
her eyes
soft
as the earth

I didn't want
to stop
hearing her
I didn't want
the words
to run out

I loved
her laughter
like bells
how it rang
from the place
of sadness

she came
naked
and my hands
rose
like birds
from a tree

I dreamed
the lovely one
and she
dreamed me
a silver bracelet
on her wrist

dawn

streetlamp leaning
into the early morning's light
buckled pavement
and broken glass

last night's commerce
litters wellington
and bannatyne
doorways lit
by the sun

city's going down

collapsing
into its own memory

empty streets
and the fluttering wings
of the 6 a.m. angel
ascending

blow wind blow